Fact & Memory

Keith Dow
Tyler Carroll

Printed in the United States of America
ISBN 13: 978-0-578-44264-8 (paperback)
Publisher: Dead Reckoning Collective, LLC

Book cover designed by: Tyler Carroll & Keith Dow
Book cover photo credit: Christopher Adams

For signed copies visit www.deadreckoningco.com

DEDICATION

This is for those who have something to say but have not yet said it.

To our family and friends - it is our hope that you can understand and relate to the experiences and impressions among these pages.

Foreword

Someone once asked me, "Where are all the poets these days?"

I responded, "They got wise and started writing songs."

From Enheduanna to Bob Dylan to Chino Marino, the undeniable truth is that music and poetry have been intertwined for as long as the two mediums have existed.

While not completely necessary to appreciation the craft, it is helpful to understand that poetry, like music, is a combination of art and literature. Some poetry is abstract in nature, inviting the reader to interpret meaning based on their own experiences, ultimately "completing" the work, while other poetry is much more literal in nature.

Currently there exists an image of poetry as a feminine expression of emotion, a frail exploration of feelings that many men would prefer to avoid. Granted, the genre has recently been primarily occupied by softly spoken souls pining over lost love and painted with the soft tears of victimhood. There is, however, an emergence of power and strength forged in rugged ink, penned with the grit of an austere human experience.

The collaborative efforts of Keith Dow's heavy, punching pen and Tyler Carroll's melodic tempo create a resulting collection of lyrical expression that can only come from walking some of life's most challenging roads. As such, *Fact and Memory* feels as close to an early, A Day to Remember album as a collection of Bukowski. Every poem has a tempo and a rhythm all on its own, yet a continuity exists from track to track.

The more I think about the aforementioned question, the more I believe the great poets of our generation have been right here in front of us all along. Filling their cups with whiskey and metal, burning their wars that we may remember. Men like David Rose, Justin Eggen, Jonathan Baxter, Keith Dow, and Tyler Carroll are forging a new sound from an otherwise ebbing genre.

Can you hear it?
A collective, emerging.
A dormant genre, resurging.
Set to the fierce beat
of soldier's feet, marching.

This isn't an anthology, poem after poem
It's a metal core album, played on a war-drum,
with aggression, where words become weapons
and life lessons from new bastions-
literature from experience.
where men, born as poets, went into the world
discovered the worst of us, the best of us,
and brought it back home for the rest of us.
so we could know how living feels, how dying feels
How real men stand at a time when masculine
is a dirty word - faux antonym of civility.

Here is prospective of suffering and prosperity
The backbone of frailty, broken
Lived, written, and spoken
in the language of reality
This poetry is the melody
of *Fact and Memory*.

Get ready for the breakdown.

-Leo Jenkins

Introduction

Fact and memory both play a pivotal role in storytelling. There has to be a perfect balance for both, but unlike other crafts there is no formula. Each story is different and some require the truth to be bent more than others. This becomes more complicated when sharing a narrative. Sometimes the way we remember an event is different than the way it transpired and sometimes the way an event is documented does not accurately represent the chain of events, which actually occurred.

Writing these poems reminded us that facts can be tailored, omitted or embellished and memories can be repressed, distorted or forgotten all together. In that respect, we aimed to remember the forgotten and to contend misconceptions. We avoided claiming truth because the attached notion of judgment. However, we felt obligated to remind people the complications with subjectivity in a world, where people define reality as perception. If there is a singular truth the means of obtaining it is through a collective story.

Vietnam War veteran and critically acclaimed author, Tim O'Brien said "Stories are for joining the past to the future. Stories are for those late hours in the night when you can't remember how you got from where you were to where you are. Stories are for eternity, when memory is erased, when there is nothing to remember except the story."

These poems are about our journeys through life as we have experienced it to date. Traveling through relationships and conflicts with love, hate, happiness and growth. The vast majority of these experiences involve other human beings and our perspective is only a sliver of any given story, but these are ours to share and we hope you can relate to them on some level.

-KD & TC

Fact & Memory

Sometimes the two perfectly coincide
Sometimes separated by miles and miles
At times the obstacle is geographic
At times temporal logic is absent
There are times it's a matter of when
There are times when it's all that matters
Often times what we believe we lived different
Often times what we remember just isn't

-KD & TC-

The Divide

Do you really want to get to know us?
We're the kids that played in the middle of the street
From throwing eggs at houses
To throwing grenades at houses
We toed the line and swore an oath.
We toed the line and swore them off
Bent rules to keep a standard
With enough income to keep us hammered
And the action was relaxing
But the silence brought the violence
And the smoke
And the dirt
And the blood
And when we returned
Everything was clean
And became a routine
And echoes from broken records
Sound a lot like bitchin'
But y'all weren't there
And y'all will never understand
Because y'all don't ask
And we don't explain
We're too distant for friendships
And too close for most
Uncomfortable conversations
Aren't meant for acquaintances

-TC-

Edwin

The violence sets us apart
Chasms in conversation
With men who've never raised fists
With women impervious to this
Watched a man take a knife before I could drive
Watched what human beings could cope with
And skulls cave in
And retinas are detached
And orbital bones
And ribs
Break like dollar store toys

-KD-

Tree of Life

A Tree of Life with roots of evil
Will die in the storm before it's ever born.
The sun is its father, but it's raised by mother earth
If it soaks up knowledge it will survive its birth.
Sprouting ideas and growing its spirit.
There's a whisper in the wind, be quiet and you can hear it.
Doesn't need to fear when the weather gets cloudy
It knows its true colors and reveals them proudly.
It isn't shy because when it looks around.
It realizes every tree is similar just different branches in the ground.
All waiting to be found.
Discovered and loved. Nourished by nature
Its reflection has become its only true stranger.
Covered with bark to hide the inner
Shadowed by the dark and transforms to a sinner.
A stump at worst and a home at best.
Too much in between to explain the rest.
Now let it be known when the red leaf falls
It the end of a season for no apparent reason.
Time to change its ways - over countless days
Give it time to mature to reach its full potential.
It sounds so simple yet gets complicated
When it timbers down something new is created.
Seed to sprout it has conquered the drought
And a shout of thunder finally made it to wonder.
"Why am I here and what is my purpose?"
"You're a tree, my child, you must first get rooted, then nourish
Those around you, so the whole would can flourish."

-TC-

Ode to Love American

We worshipped the words
The music came second
Caught up in convictions
Lessened by life lessons
Records remain but
No longer living those lyrics
Still standing out with
Shreds of the same spirit
Making out in backseats to babies in car seats
Kept friendships on shelves
Some hardly have a heartbeat
Growing up was selling out
But we're still listening "to the sound
of breaking down and breaking out."[1]

-KD-

[1] Wesley Eisold, Give Up The Ghost. *We're Down Til We're Underground*, Equal Vision Records, 2003.

Poke the Bear

Regardless,
If there is shit on my face
Or if it is just the fly's nature,
Its presence tests my patience.
I'll be bound to swing
Eventually.

Restless Soul

"Restless soul,
this place will never be your home."[2]
Aimless drone,
Did they promise you a home?
Ways of old,
They dug your six holes.
Nameless stones,
Came back and said heaven's cold.
Hell is home,
Take this time to mend those bones.
Send a note,
They're patiently waiting for words of hope.
Pay the toll,
Fund the road, running for wandering ghosts.

-KD-

Jeffrey Eaton, Modern Life Is War. *Witness*, Deathwish Inc, 2005.

Attention Deficit

Like a flick from a Bic
The spark comes as easy as it goes.
Undivided attention
Is built on the banks of a river,
And erodes
As fast the stream flows.
A handful sand
During the construction of a castle.
The tide is coming
To destroy an idea;
My boat is sinking
And I'm up creek without a paddle.

Deliver Us

Our brothers who art in heaven
Too Many be thy name

Blend in

A chameleon doesn't even
Feel comfortable in his skin
Can be anything he wants
If only he wanted to be him
Self-reflection
Can mirror a resemblance of deception
Broken glass, half truths
Bottled up depression
A release of relapse
Unmasks transgressions
Against reason and nature
The future
Past and present
Continuum of change
Weakens and strengthens
The will to fight for
Writing wrongs I've mistaken
The luxury of rest
Lies within the risen
The scales of our skin
Are the bars to our soul's prison.

-TC-

Just

Lately I see no sense in it
Abandoned books littered with penmanship

Typography

The contour lines of written words
Can birth a mountain out of ink.
The contrast of white and black
Creates the light that hides
Under the canopies
That dances with shade
Deep in the valleys.
A fork in the road
Leads a traveler
To the left or right.
A poet on the road
Is left to write
Beyond actuality.
Cursive is persuasive
Unifying characters into one.
Bridges have been built
As walls have fallen down.
Conflicts resolve,
New chronicles begin,
Renovated worlds
Are authored on these pages.
And at the expense of trees
We can dream about a forest.

-TC-

Jody

You can't condemn broomsticks next to front doors
When you've left red chem lights next to yours
Unsorted, unwanted
Unwelcome, forgotten
Exchange fleeting, sad little vows with
The same cheating, traveling spouses
You can't blame her, you can't blame him
For failing to stand for something that was already caving in

-KD-

Direction

Speak up

Look out

Dig in

Get down

Go right

Push forward

Don't be

Left behind

Ours

You're "Wild Horses"
Radio comes in and out
I am "Simple Man"

Judge's Robe

The verdict is in
And the gavel is heavy
Twelve strangers' opinions
Label me what I am
Regardless of the truth
Perception paints the picture
I don't care what people think
That's a lie
I do
That's my crime
And they know
I'm guilty

-TC-

Faces, Not Names

Two in twelve months
Blue collars for nooses

Hancock

I've surrounded myself by men
Who've played a supportive role,
But they're the hero
In someone else's action flick.
My comedy, their tragedy
The suspense is alleviated
By the punchline.
Mountain top cliff hangers
Have us sitting on the edge.
I remember, they forget
What it feels like to fly.
Climatic endings
Twist the imagination amok,
While optimism spills out of
A glass half empty.
I'm thirsty for adventure
And my companions need revival.
We're listening for our calling
But our headphones are in.

-TC-

Home

We made homes
We built homes
We left home
We missed home
We dreamt home
We wrote home
We got home
We broke home
We lost home
We lost home

-KD-

Protesters

There's so many problems in this world!
                    Be sure to shout louder
There needs to be change!
                    Be sure to shout louder
We must do something!
                    Be sure to shout louder
My heart is weak,
My throat is sore,
And no one is listening!
                    You should have shouted louder

The Trap

Heads up
It's a setup
They thrive on turmoil
We dine on snake oil

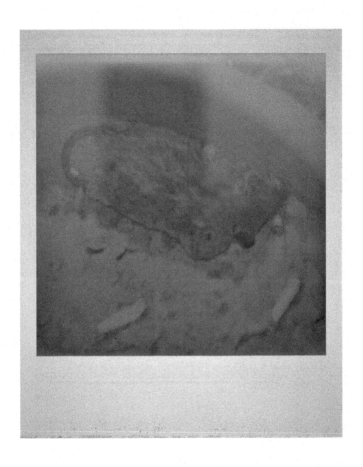

Countdown

Long for
Three sides
To uphold
One truth

Run Tell

Stay among the ones who made you men
They love you and you love them
Slay the ones who threaten their health
They were there when you laughed and wept
Aim to stay in heaven half an hour and no less
Away from hell before they tell the devil of your death

-KD-

Discrepancy

We gave up freedom
To fight for freedom.
We made a promise
For the land of promise.
We longed for war
To be left in war.
We were the youth
Unrelated to the youth.
We despised the entitled
To become the entitled.
We know sacrifice
So others have no sacrifice.
We are living heroes
Amongst dead heroes.
We appreciate silence
Only to avoid the silence.

-KD-

Forever War

Toddlers were fought for
Never knew the towers though
Now babies fight wars

Digging our Graves

To take a stand on a hill
Leads to countless killings and deaths
Needless or honorable
What's not debatable are breaths
Taken and recycled
Carbon dated now a fossil
History repeats itself
And no one is responsible?
Ignorant to patterns
Woven in a fabric of sequence
Unaccountable authority
Leaves the masses with knees bent
Grazing fields
Of forced fed pleasures
Undiscovered contentment
Of what matters and measures
Up to expectation
A hesitation to fall
Into a pit with a shovel
Filled with us all

-TC-

Timeless Violence

God bless the dead and
Blessed are the fighters
And their legacies' remnants
Of timeless violence, silent miles
Through what they prayed
Were abandoned landscapes
But not a thing is promised
Except a hole and a coffin

-KD-

Cognitively Influential

Our span of reach has widened
Our attention span has narrowed
If change happened in a moment
I doubt that we would notice
Too focused on the past
Justifying could've, would've, should've
Relying on a promise of the future
But Father Time is a liar
The fresh has become stale
In matter of seconds
Break the wrist of the hand
That dictates when the sunsets
When we write the rules
The ink isn't permanent
We don't believe in what we see
We creatively interpret it

-TC-

The House of the Rising Son

There is a house in a college town
Home to a rising son
And it was almost the ruin of one poor boy
And God, I know I was him

My mother was a gas lighter
Conflict, she was drawn to it
My father was a family man
Down in Massachusetts

Now the only thing a family man needs
Is more hours in the work week
And the only time he's satisfied
Is when the children are asleep

Oh fathers, tell your sons
Not to do what you have done
Spend your years in stress and debt
In the house of the rising son

Well, I got one foot on a trip overseas
The other foot on Main Street
But I'll always be goin' back to New Hampshire
To wear that burden all the same

Well, there is a house in a college town
Home to a rising son
And it was the ruin of one poor boy
And God, I know I am him

-KD-

God Bless America

In the beginning was the Word
And the Word was His
And man must be deaf
To let his country end up like this
We're in war torn lands
Stitching them with democratic fabrics
While we're busting at the seams
With domestic addicts
Food, drugs, porn,
And a lust for entertainment
Gluttonous distractions
Are barriers to human engagement
It's hard to love thy neighbor
When you don't know his name
You have weeds in your yard
Is he the one to blame?
An individualistic ideology
Enforced on a global scale
Impractically implemented
And good intentions pave the road to hell
We must be sure to wear a helmet
Bible-thumpers are ready
To preach the gospel and truth
Without realizing man's judgement is deadly.

-TC-

Bukowski, Billy Currington, and Chesty Puller Walk into a Bar

I think a lot about a country song
About beer and God
And men sharing thoughts on bar stools
About women and war
And how I never listened or paid attention to the lyrics
And how I never listened to women
And how I never paid much attention to what war meant
To anyone
But me

-KD-

Sin

I confess
My finesse
In archery
Is a mess

Breaking ~~Cycles~~

Empty bottles and short wrinkled remnants of cigarettes
Is what the sun comes up over and illuminates and
All of my best friends who treat girlfriends and wives like shit
All the lives I have touched and have in turn touched me
Amount to means to ends that resemble my own life like this

-KD-

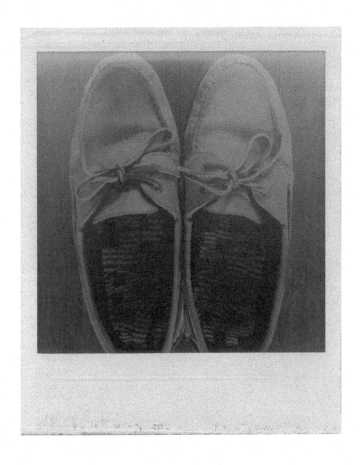

Volunteer

Kiss goodbye to my last ditch effort
The shirt off my back is in your hands
But you're still not satisfied.
The mountain air is still in my lungs
And every morning my knees creak
But you're still not satisfied.
I don't aim at heads, I aim to please
And your boots dry, because you stepped on my pride
But you're still not satisfied.
A honorable discharge, federal holidays,
Discounts at checkouts, and short walk to the car
And I'm still not satisfied.

-TC-

Has Been

Miles on his face
Smiles been replaced
Lives been at stake
Now the files and the ranks
Been gone
No smokes, no stripes
No hope, no life
Those types of low lifes are
Those I've known my whole life
And so
It goes

-KD-

Gomer Pyle

My war face is a smile
It seems I have forgotten
While memories replay
With blurry peripherals
My focus is skewed
Clouded by a lens of nostalgia
The good ole days
Never recall the misery
Selective joy
Brings unexpected pain
Thrill seeking yet never obtaining
Adrenaline has now become mundane

-TC-

Casualty Nullification

They would announce them like weather updates
They came in 2's and 3's and sometimes dozens
Sons and daughters, honored
Discovering the names
Too often drawing relations
Now it's been 2 decades and the babies are waging
I don't know them
I don't know their names
I don't know their faces
I don't know if it's good or bad
I don't know whether to be happy or sad
I won't know any of them anymore
Here's to all these friends we never met
That never saw the other side of that fence

-KD-

Watering Hole

A herd of sorority girls sip lattes
in sleeveless coats of fur.
A predator emerges
through the thick brush of traffic,
and the well-groomed beard
indicates a superior bloodline.
Hyenas laugh at unsubstantial quips.
The alpha male has a bureaucratic smile.
The awkward giraffe is still finding his legs
and at those heights
he should be able to see past the mirage, but
a flaunting bird has his attention.
A liquid reflection
confirms I'm a hungry-hungry hippo.
Ears in all directions
trying to mind my business, but
the biodiversity fills my appetite
far more than coffee shop pastries.

-TC-

Thanksgiving

Good days and bad
Days just like any other
No significance other than
We weren't where we were
On the same day years ago
The day may have a name
But it changed nothing of the agenda
Turkey dinner in New Hampshire
Mission briefs in Al Hila
Worlds apart
The smiles faked on both sides
Works of art

-KD-

Third Wheel

Obey the web of lies
Spun by the internet
Antidote from the poison
A relationship with commitment
A crowd pleaser
Love is between two people, isn't it?
A fallacy - intimacy
Is no longer intimate

-TC-

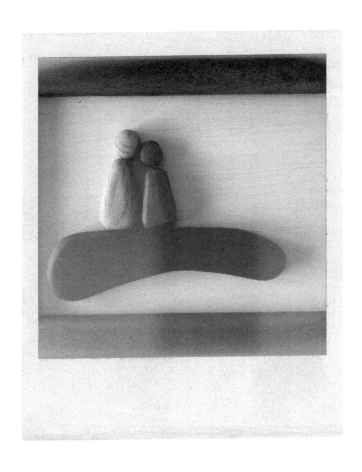

Tarp

What am I afraid of the most?
What happens when doors close
Porch lights off, deadbolts latched
Family men cocooned in with bad habits
Bundy's and Gacy's
Mistaken for
Patrons with savings
But in the spirit of Bateman
They simply are not there

-KD-

Responsibility

Father & son / Shooter & gun
Who's held responsible?
Hand & hand they walk / Hand & handle they talk
When did truth become pliable?
If lies deceit / I want to retreat
To something reliable

Subject to subjectivity / Value is in creativity
Words crash into a roadblock
Pen & paper / Responsibility of a creator
When will the judgement stop?
Better soon than later / Bitter is the flavor
Of a face without a clock

-TC-

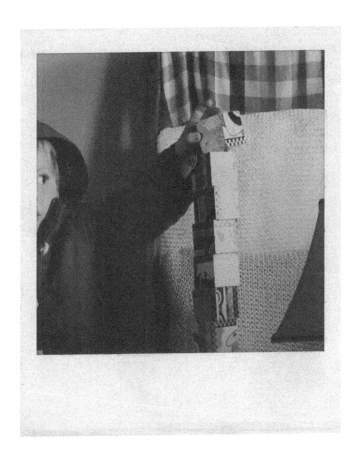

August

And you go
Sixty to zero
And then back
And in no hurry
Your bare feet
Barely touch the floor
Your hair's done
Best when you don't try
What words say
Gorgeous and perfect
How do I
Make you feel them now?

-KD-

Ryan Air

Mediterranean sands have washed over my feet
And Irish winds have combed my hair.
Austrian switchbacks remind me of snowboard crashes
But luckily the beer in Munich numbed the pain.
There are English accents that I don't understand
And my hands looked amazing while in Amsterdam.
The architecture in Paris was breathtaking
Which made it difficult to warm my hands.
But I will still eat Gelato next to the Colosseum,
Lean with the tower in the streets of Pisa,
And feel less of a man while I stand
Next to the David.
These statues and cities mean nothing to me
Unless I'm sightseeing with you.

My Friends

My friends send letters and they call
They still don't know what's going on with me at all

My friends stumble into trouble with money and the law
They might never grow up or get it together and move on

My friends found God
Sometimes I don't know if they believe in anything at all

My friends drink too much
They drink more than we did before and by themselves while
they look for true love

My friends check in to make sure I'm okay
They ask what's new and wait for me to finish like they're
rounding bases in conversation, trying to steal home plate

My friends have families
They cheat on their spouses and lie to their friends and me

My friends fake smiles and choke back tears
They forget every cigarette smoked and how we shared our
greatest hopes and fears

My friends made friends
They move from circle to circle until the next falling out is too
hard to mend

Strawberry Fields

To the point of no return
A slip away from the cliff
More like a sip away from the drift
A return is all I look for

Clarity and sobriety
Identical twins that look fraternal
Visions brought to light within the nocturnal
The stars and sun become allies

Too much to achieve
A moment changes the course of time
Alcohol dilutes feelings by silencing the mind
Why can't I think straight?

Perception is defined by *blurred* lines

Night Dogs

Lay awake
Lie and wait
Nap in a hole
Nest in my soul
Lest we forget
Less we regret
Savoring war
Say we were more
Our fathers' sons
Out on the run
Jump where we measured
Just for forever
All we were was
All that they loved
Quiet as they kept
Quarter life regrets
Guarantee me it's something else
Got to believe we've summoned hell
Read between lines
Roads to "good times"
Far from home for a time
Falling down, "I'm just fine."

-KD-

Memorial Day

My memory ain't what it was;
However
I don't need a day to remember
A man I won't forget.
Tears have been shed,
Hope has been found,
My son has his name, and
My pen is almost out of ink.
I have found, at times,
Less is more.
Silence can be an appropriate response.

Raise your Glass in Moderation

Been around the block
Now the world a little too
It's outta my system
Thinking "I'll be finished soon."
I've seen serene settings
War torn spots too
I'm ready to return home
To try to find my lost youth

-KD-

Graveyard Shift

Here's a true story
Not a Hollywood rendition.
Last night a young boy
Pinned his brother into submission.
With the intention to puncture skin,
With a blade previously hidden.
His parents brought him in
For admission.
It was the graveyard shift
And sedation was his prescription.
Nurses closed in with a needle in hand.
He kicked. He screamed.
His parents held him down.
They kissed him. He dreamed.
I wonder…
Is he in a nightmare or a better place?
A boy his age
Shouldn't be filled with such rage.
His mother cried a river,
And like a tree,
His father fell silent.
What's gone wrong in this world
To make a 9-year old so violent?
The clinician's decision
Was this kid's condition
Is fueled by lies told
In Hollywood renditions.

-TC-

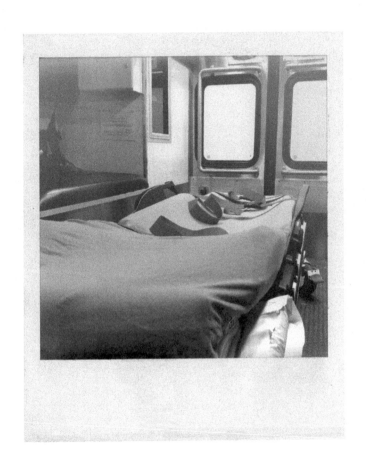

Better Man

More integrity
Spent time on many friends' floors
Ten times as many

Table Talks

Steam from a mug ignites a conversation
Red eyes, black lungs from smoke inhalation
A flame danced through the night
The roof is on fire
All we need is water
Please don't let it burn
Cool the atmosphere
The sun consumes the rain
The heat has become a drug
Charred emotions feel no pain
Torched dreams
Silent screams
Douse the haze with solid streams
A band of brothers tangled in the inferno
Silenced the devil until tomorrow.

-TC-

The Knot

Warmth of other suns
Warmth of other sons
That old verse about a snail on a razor
That old verse about fences and neighbors
Conversations with basement bar patrons
Conversations with philosophy in layman's
Rats wriggle around on subway tracks
Rats wriggle around ruining what they had

-KD-

Oak St.

On a bench, on a bench
I sit here and wait
For someone to entertain me
I am still unamused
As I sit here and wait
On a bench, on a bench

On a bench, on a bench
I ponder and reflect
On what tomorrow shall bring me
I may never know
As I ponder and reflect
On a bench, on a bench

On a bench, on a bench
I adjust and stretch
Chronic ailments from betters days
I don't move like I use to
As I adjust and stretch
On a bench, on a bench

On a bench, on a bench
I close my eyes and rest
Create and destroy forgotten lands
I escape my limitations
As I close my eyes and rest
On a bench, on a bench

-TC-

120

You listened to me and you let me listen to you
When there was no one else or no one else I wanted to
When the ones I wanted didn't want me
When the ones who didn't want me
You didn't have all the answers but you gave me just enough
To find them on my own
The tragedy is no one could appreciate you
Your dings, scratches and dents
The demos
The duplicates
The compilations
The EP's
The playlists
The full lengths from CD's
Every song that rocked me to sleep
While at war
Abroad with an enemy
At home with myself
I hope the meth was worth it
I hope your tent is warm
I wish you could have heard it
This open letter about an iPod that carried me through war

-KD-

Pay Attention

Register a note
Validation is through change
Inevitable inflation
Marks up perception
Without an attached title to claim

You can't bullshit a bullshitter
Appearance is pursued through wealth
Waging war against identity
Bankrupts integrity
Dust settled failures expose oneself

Invest your time on your mind
The root of all evil is greed
Unquenched palates
Feed orchestrated ballots
Counterfeit promises become currency

-TC-

Home is Where the Headstone is

I drove past the family plot;
Stones protruding through snow
Over the homes of their ghosts

A New Heart

A hope filled heart
A wandering mind
A restful life
With sleepless nights
Open eyes I see
Darkness in me
Closed eyes I feel
A light that's real
What can I hold onto
As I am pulled under?
In an awaken nightmare
In a dreamful slumber
What cross do I bear
If the weight's been lifted?
What treasure do I seek
That have not be gifted?

-TC-

Death Comes

I have been 1 of 6 gripping casket handles
Death comes to visit us all
I have told anyone listening that I am still standing
Death comes to visit us all
I have wished them well across the great divide
Death comes to visit us all
I have thanked and I have cursed for what I have seen in my time
Death comes to visit us all
I have felt absolutely nothing like a heavy black blanket
Death comes to visit us all
A man said he should tremble to take us
But Death still comes to visit us all

-KD-

Good Weather

As a matter of control
Let's stroll down memory lane
I hate backseat driving
But I love to look out the window
Trees pass
And I know they'll eventually fall
And that a Captain will go down with his ship
No question at all
What about the passengers?
A silent or violent protest
Won't contest the situation at all
So enjoy the ride
At least the sky
Is blue.

-TC-

GLOSSARY

Go
Live
Outside
So
Strangers
Aren't
Reigning over
You

-KD-

Fact

Flirting with fiction
Hurling predictions
"I am the only victim"
As the amputee limps in

Accept the deception
Reject the exception
Bodies lie in collections
When opportunity steps in

My first full notebook
Versus my worst words spoken
My heart was homeless
My plate was loaded

I contested the norm
Since I was born and sworn in
Longed for home with my Lord
But found none in a land so foreign

-KD & TC-

&

It's unkind times and unforgiving timelines
And it's knees that ache when it rains
And it's suicide hotlines
And it's bottles without bottoms

It's living paycheck to paycheck without praise
And it's the end of month bank statements
And it's paying too much damn taxes
And it's playing keeping up with the Jones'

It's the shots of Jameson on the bar
And it's the ones standing in front of them
And it's the ones we raise those tiny glasses to
And it's tattoos of helmets atop rifles with boots

It's not enough hours in a day
And it's "I'm too tired"
And it's "I will get to that later"
And it's my plans tomorrow that I had no say in

It's the dirt I wanna stay on the safe side of
And it's the towns and cities I've been to but never more
And it's the highways, backroads and billboards
And it's backyards where there was a life before

It's flying too close to the sun
And it's a fear of fire and burns and brimstone
And it's losing sleep chasing dreams
And it's pulling over with a tank half full

It's choosing to reminisce instead of choosing to live
And it's the same phone calls and catching up on bullshit
And it's the time between
And it's the times we shared
And it's the time we spent
And it's the time it took to figure out how we ever slept

It's pondering what could have been
And it's the balance on mercy's scale
And it's the things I've felt
And it's the hands I've dealt
And it's the hardships we've shared
And it's the moment of clarity that I can still feel something

-KD & TC-

Memory

A needle in haystack
A debt I can't payback
Pulled from thin air
Like words I can't take back

The "good old days" were sometimes
Not so good and void of sunshine
When every point is "remember that one time?"
It was one big joke and I was the punch line

Seen as a hero felt like a masked villain
Courageous men resembling children
Kept a dream alive by way of maiming and killing
Why dig graves without intentions to fill them?

-TC & KD-

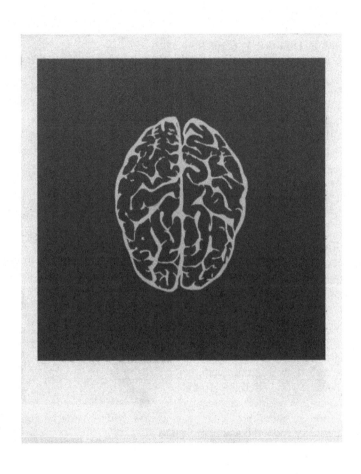

Keith Dow

Keith Dow is a born New Englander, who has been writing ever since he could hold a pen. He spent 5 years on active duty in the US Army before being honorably discharged in 2013 to start a family. At this point, Keith is best known for being the only US Army veteran living in Canada with A-M-E-R-I-C-A-N tattooed across his knuckles.

Tyler Carroll

Tyler Carroll comes from a military family and bounced around during his youth. After a failed attempt at college he decided to become a Medic for US Army. After his service he and his wife returned to Texas, and he became a firefighter and father. Writing is a recently found passion, but Tyler has always had a wide-ranging curiosity and a diligent approach to life.

133

Made in USA - Kendallville, IN
1225390_9780578442648